The Nature Kid's Guide to

CICADAS

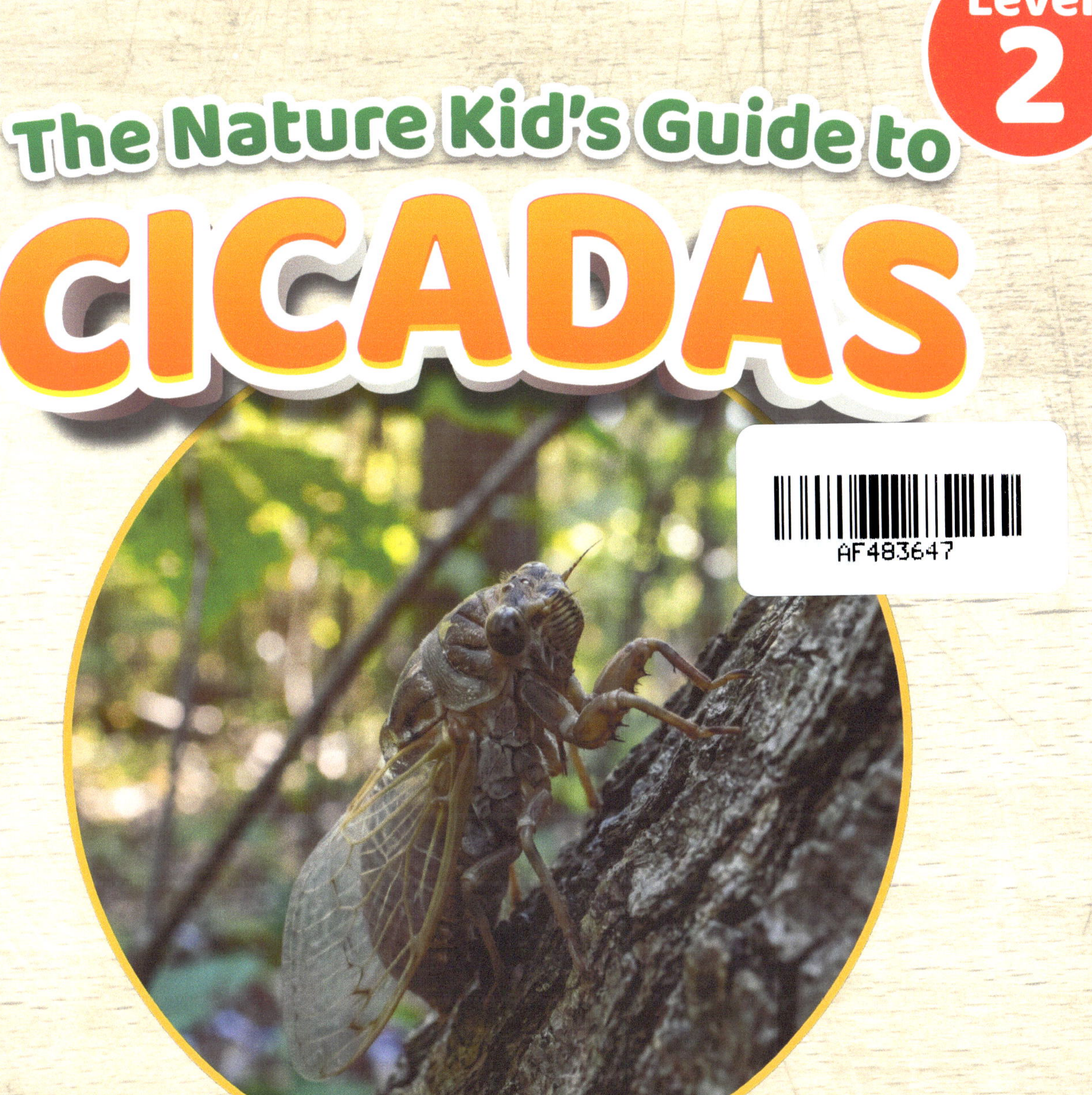

DAVID ANDERSON

LP Media Inc. Publishing
Text copyright © 2026 by LP Media Inc.
All rights reserved.

For information address LP Media Inc. Publishing,
30012 Variolite St NW, Princeton MN 55371
www.lpmedia.org

Publication Data

Cicadas
The Nature Kid's Guide to Cicadas — First edition.

Summary: "Learn all about Cicadas, the Nature Kid Way"
— Provided by publisher.

ISBN: 979-8-89818-249-6

[1. Cicadas – Non-Fiction] I. Title.

Title: The Nature Kid's Guide to Cicadas

CONTENTS

TREE TIME

DID YOU KNOW?
There are more than 3,000 kinds of cicadas buzzing around the world — but most look so alike that even experts get confused!

Buzzzzz! A cicada clings to rough bark and starts to sing.

Cicadas are insects that love trees. You can find them in forests, parks, and backyards. They spend most of their lives near trees.

These bugs hold tight to bark with tiny hooked claws. They like warm places with lots of sun. Oaks, maples, and pines all make great homes for them.

Some cicadas live where it gets very hot. Others prefer cooler spots with mild weather. If there are trees, cicadas feel right at home.

WORLD WIDE

One rare cicada species lives only in the Sacramento Mountains of New Mexico — found nowhere else on Earth!

Whirrrr! A cicada lands on a tree in a warm forest in Australia.

Cicadas live on six of the seven continents. You can hear them in Asia, Africa, and Europe. They buzz in North and South America too.

Australia has some of the loudest types on Earth. Rain forests in warm lands hold tiny ones no bigger than your fingernail. Even hot, dry deserts have cicadas hiding in the few trees that grow there.

The only place with no cicadas is Antarctica. It is way too cold and has no trees. Cicadas need warm weather and trees to survive.

BIG AND SMALL

One of the smallest cicadas, Mogannia minuta, is just a half an inch long — it could sit on your fingertip!

Crrrick! A big cicada stretches its wide wings in the warm sun.

Most cicadas are about 1-2 inches long. That is about as long as your pinky finger. Some are bigger, and some are much smaller.

The Empress cicada is the largest kind in the world. With wings spread, it measures 8 inches across—as wide as a small bird! It lives in the rain forests of Asia.

Most cicadas you spot are about the size of your thumb. They look big when they fly past your face. But their bodies are actually quite light.

BODY BUZZ

Cicadas have five eyes! Two are big compound eyes, and three are tiny simple eyes on top of the head.

10

Click! A cicada bends its belly and makes a sharp, buzzing pop.

A cicada has six legs, big eyes, and four clear wings. Its body has three main parts: a head, a middle, and a belly.

Males have a special part called a **tymbal**. It sits on the belly and works like a tiny drum. The tymbal clicks up to 400 times per second to make that loud buzz!

Cicadas also have a thin tube called a beak. They poke it into plants to drink. It works like a tiny straw.

SUPER SENSE
FUN FACT!
Cicadas hear sounds through a thin patch of skin stretched tight on their belly!
12

Zzzzzip! A cicada feels the warm soil and crawls out of its hole.

Cicadas use their senses to stay safe. Their big eyes can see almost all the way around them. They spot birds and other dangers fast.

These bugs can also feel shaking in trees and the ground. A cicada can tell when something big is coming close. Then it gets ready to fly away.

Under the dirt, young cicadas feel the soil get warm each spring. That tells them the season has changed. They wait for it to get exactly the right temperature, then they know it is time to dig up and start a new life above ground.

HIDE HARD

Cicada wings have tiny spikes that kill germs on contact—like a built-in germ shield!

DID YOU KNOW?

Shhhhh! A green cicada sits very still and blends into a leaf.

Cicadas are not fast runners or strong fighters. So they hide instead! Their colors help them blend in with bark and leaves.

Brown cicadas look just like tree bark. Green ones vanish against fresh leaves. When a bird comes close, the cicada holds perfectly still and waits.

Some cicadas flash their bright wings at hunters. The sudden surprise gives them time to fly away. This quick trick can save their lives.

SIP
SAP

DID YOU KNOW?

Cicadas pee a lot! They squirt out streams of extra water while they drink—sometimes right on people below!

Slurrrp! A cicada pokes its beak into a branch and drinks sweet sap.

Cicadas do not eat solid food at all. They only drink! They poke their beak into a tree and sip the sweet sap that flows inside.

Sap is a watery liquid that moves through trees. It gives cicadas all the sugar and water they need. One cicada can sip from the same spot for hours without moving.

Young cicadas under the ground drink sap too. They tap into tree roots deep in the soil. From egg to adult, sap is all a cicada ever needs to eat.

SING LOUD

A male cicada has to turn off its own hearing when it sings, or the noise would damage its ears!

REEEE! A male cicada fills the summer air with a buzzing song.

Only male cicadas sing. Their songs are the loudest sounds any insect can make. A single buzz can go on for minutes without stopping.

Each kind of cicada has its own special song. Some buzz, some whine, and some chirp. A male sings to tell females he is nearby and ready to mate.

A singing cicada can reach 100 **decibels**—as loud as a lawn mower right next to your ear! Imagine that sound outside your window. On hot days, whole neighborhoods fill with song.

WATCH OUT

DID YOU KNOW?
People in many countries eat cicadas as a crunchy, protein-packed snack!

Swoop! A hungry bird dives down — the cicada flies away fast!

Many animals love to eat cicadas. Birds, squirrels, and spiders all hunt them. Even dogs and cats will snap up a cicada that lands nearby.

Wasps are one of the scariest hunters of all. A cicada killer wasp can grab a cicada right out of the air. It stings the cicada and carries it back to its nest to feed its babies.

Fish eat cicadas that fall into water. Ants swarm ones that land on the ground. With so many hungry hunters, cicadas must always watch out.

SUN SONGS

DID YOU KNOW?
Cicadas only start singing when the air temperature hits at least 72 degrees — below that, they stay completely silent!

Drrrrrr! A cicada warms up its body and begins its noon call.

On hot summer days, cicadas are very busy. They sing the most when the sun is high and warm. As the air heats up, the songs get louder and louder.

By late morning, the buzzing starts. Cicadas spend the middle of the day singing, resting, and sipping sap. They sit on warm bark soaking up the sun.

When evening comes, the songs slow down. Most cicadas go quiet at night. They save their energy for another hot, noisy day ahead.

CROWD CHORUS

Cicadas do not bite or sting. They are completely safe for people to pick up and hold!

REEEEEE! Thousands of cicadas sing together from every tree.

Cicadas are not loners. Many kinds come out at the exact same time. When they do, they form huge, noisy groups called choruses.

A **chorus** can have millions of cicadas packed into one small area. Large choruses can cover dozens of acres of forest — the sound overlaps so much it becomes one continuous wall of noise!

Being in a big group helps keep cicadas safe. With millions around, birds simply cannot eat them all. There are always more cicadas than any hunter could catch.

LOVE SONGS

Some female cicadas pick their mate based on how loud his song is—the louder, the better!

Chirrrp! A female cicada flicks her wings to answer a singing male.

Male cicadas sing to call a mate. The song has to be just right. If it is not, the female will simply fly away.

When she hears a song she likes, she flicks her wings to make a clicking sound. The click tells the male exactly where she is. He follows the sound through the branches to find her.

After they mate, the male goes right back to singing. He wants to find more mates before summer ends. He will sing until his last day.

TINY NYMPHS

DID YOU KNOW?

Within minutes of hatching, a cicada nymph has already found its way to the ground and started digging!

Crack! Tiny cicada nymphs hatch and crawl out of the tree branch.

A female cicada cuts small slits in a tree branch with a sharp part of her body. She lays her eggs inside the wood. One mother can lay up to 600 eggs!

The eggs rest quietly in the branch for a few weeks. Then they hatch. Tiny babies called **nymphs** come out. Each one is barely bigger than a grain of rice.

The new nymphs do not look much like cicadas yet. They have no wings and no song. But they are tough little animals, and their journey is just beginning.

GROW SOLO

Some cicada nymphs dig down as deep as eight feet underground!

Plop! A nymph lands in the dirt and begins to dig all alone.

Once the eggs hatch, the nymphs are completely on their own. Their mother flew away long ago. There are no lessons, no help, and no one showing them what to do.

Each tiny nymph drops from the branch and hits the ground. Then it does something remarkable — it starts to dig. Its front legs are built for pushing through soil, and within seconds it is gone.

Just like that, the nymph disappears underground and does not come back up for years.

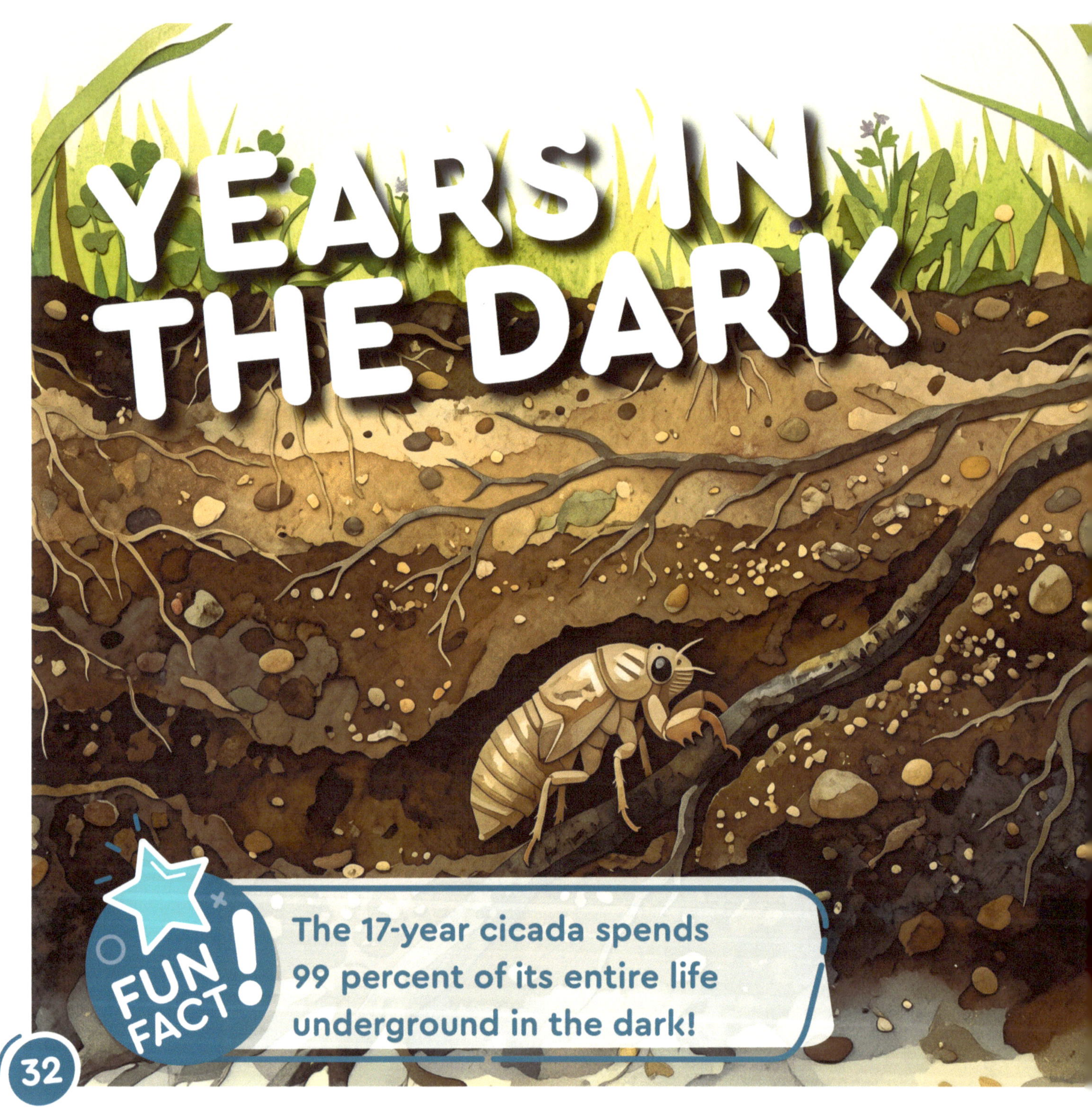

YEARS IN THE DARK
FUN FACT!
The 17-year cicada spends 99 percent of its entire life underground in the dark!

Drip. Deep underground, a cicada nymph sips a root and slowly grows.

Most cicadas spend a few years underground before coming up. But some spend 13 or 17 years down there. That is longer than most kids have been alive.

Down in the dark, a nymph does not do much. It finds a tree root, pokes in its beak, and sips. Then it waits. Year after year, it slowly grows. It sheds its skin five times as it gets bigger.

Why 13 years or 17 years exactly? Both are prime numbers — numbers that cannot be divided evenly. Scientists think this confuses predators. No animal can time its own life cycle to match a prime number.

THE BIG DAY

DID YOU KNOW?
During a mass emergence, there can be more than one million cicadas packed into a single acre of land!

Rumble! On one warm spring night, millions of cicadas push up through the ground all at once.

After years underground, every cicada in the area feels the same thing — the soil hits 64 degrees. That is the signal. Then, at the same time, millions of them push up through the ground together.

By morning, trees are covered. The noise is so loud people can hear it inside their homes with the windows shut.

Scientists call this a **mass emergence**. It happens once, it is enormous, and then it is over. The cicadas that waited the longest put on the biggest show of all.

SHORT SUMMER

Pop! A fresh cicada sits on its empty shell and looks out at the world for the very first time.

After climbing up from the ground, a cicada grips a tree and breaks free from its old skin one last time. It leaves behind a hollow brown shell — a perfect copy of its old body, right down to the tiny claws.

The new adult stretches its wings and waits for them to dry. Then it joins the chorus. It sings, finds a mate, and lays its eggs.

All of that happens in just two to six weeks. After up to 17 years of waiting, a cicada's time above ground is very short.

SPOT SHELLS

Most cicada shells are found between one and five feet up a tree trunk — right at eye level for most kids!

Look! A perfect brown cicada shell clings to the tree bark.

Cicadas are easy to find on a warm summer day. Just step outside and listen! Their loud songs will lead you right to them.

Look at tree trunks for empty brown shells. Cicadas leave these behind when they break free and become adults. You can pick them up and look closely—they are crunchy and hollow inside.

The best time to look is on hot mornings in June or July. Check trees in parks and yards. With a bit of patience, you can spot a live cicada and watch it sing!

GLOSSARY

nymph
A young cicada that has not yet grown its wings.

tymbal
A part on a male cicada's belly that clicks to make sound.

decibel
A unit used to measure how loud a sound is.

chorus
A big group of cicadas all singing at the same time.

mass emergence
When millions of cicadas all come out of the ground at exactly the same time after years underground.